Let's Put the Sweets on the Tray

To Parents: Your child can place the cakes anywhere on the tray. This activity builds hand-eye coordination.

Cut out the sweets and glue them to the tray.

Let's Pretend to Be Animals

To Parents: Encourage your child to use his or her body and voice to imitate the animals. It encourages creativity and expression. (And it's fun!)

Pretend you are each animal by making the animal sounds.

Glue   Glue   Glue

Let's Trace the Curves

To Parents: This activity builds handwriting skills through practice with gently curving lines. Your child can use a pencil or crayon to trace the dotted lines.

GOOD JOB!
Sticker

Help the sea creatures swim. Trace the ▦ ▦ ▦ from ➡ to ➡.

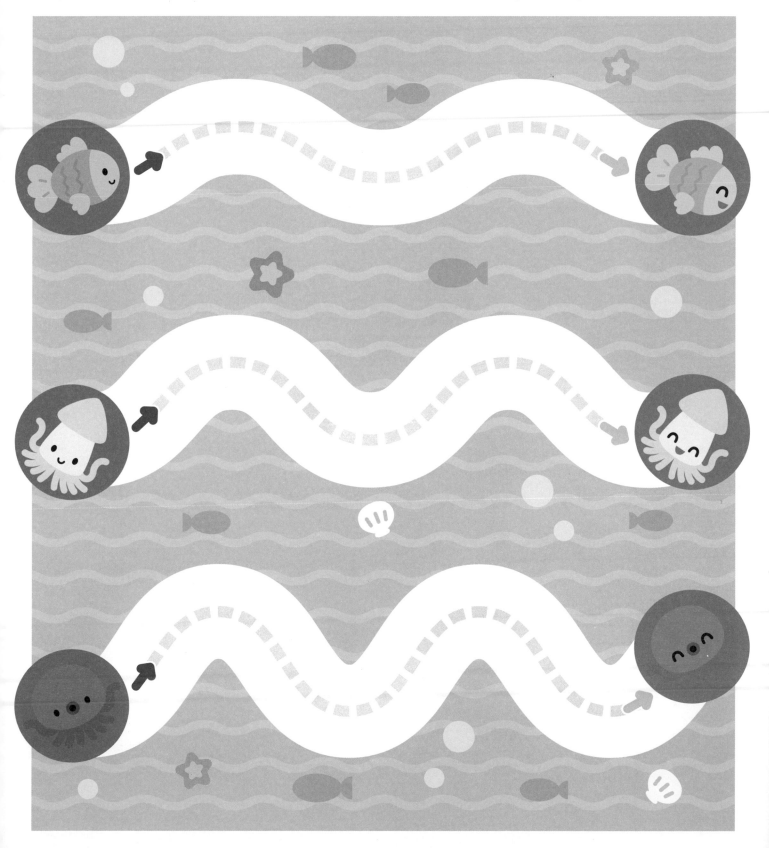

Let's Color the Shapes

GOOD JOB!

Sticker

Color the white shapes with matching colors.

Red

Example

Yellow

Green

Orange

Let's Glue the Foods in Place

To Parents: Your child can place the food anywhere on the plate, but the food should stay inside the plate. Cutting and gluing exercise hand-eye coordination.

Cut out the foods and glue them to the bear-shaped plate. Find the cherry sticker in the front of the book. Put it on the food it fits best.

• Example •

Let's Color the Shapes

To Parents: This activity focuses on the differences among colors. After your child finishes coloring, ask for the name of each color.

Color the white shapes with the matching colors.

Blue

Example

Green

Red

Pink

Glue   Glue   Glue   Glue

Let's Find the Matches

To Parents: In this activity, your child will recognize the differences among objects. Call attention to the colors and shapes of each item.

GOOD JOB!

Sticker

Which objects are the same?

Draw a line from ➡ to each matching object.

Let's Draw a Matching Rocket

To Parents: Show your child the picture in the example box. Then, ask your child to pay attention to the location, length, and direction of each line needed to finish the picture. Connecting the dots in this puzzle helps develop handwriting skills. It also exercises your child's observational skills.

GOOD JOB!

Sticker

Draw lines from ● to ● to make a rocket picture that matches the example.

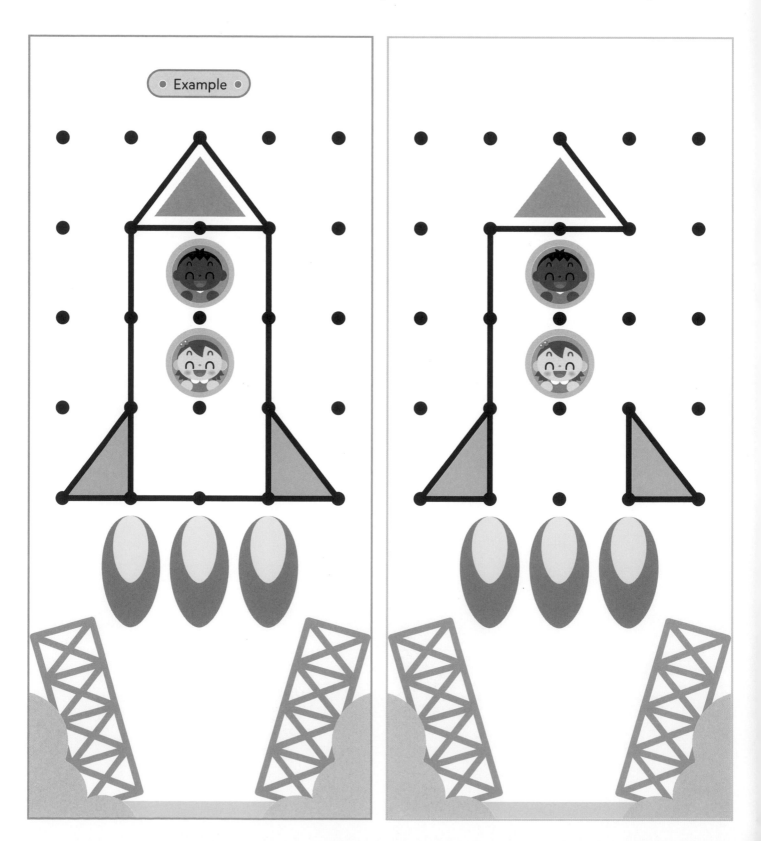

● Example ●

Let's Glue the Hair in Place

To Parents: This activity exercises fine motor skills and creativity. Point out the examples below. Your child may cut the paper in a single piece or in many pieces that can be arranged into a unique hair style.

Cut out the paper below to look like hair. Glue it on the child's head. Then, put the ribbon or hat stickers on top.

• Example •

• Example •

Let's Find the Same Shapes

To Parents: Here, your child will practice telling the differences among objects. Call attention to the characteristics of each shape.

Find the □, △, and ○ in the picture below.
Then, draw a line connecting each shape to its match.

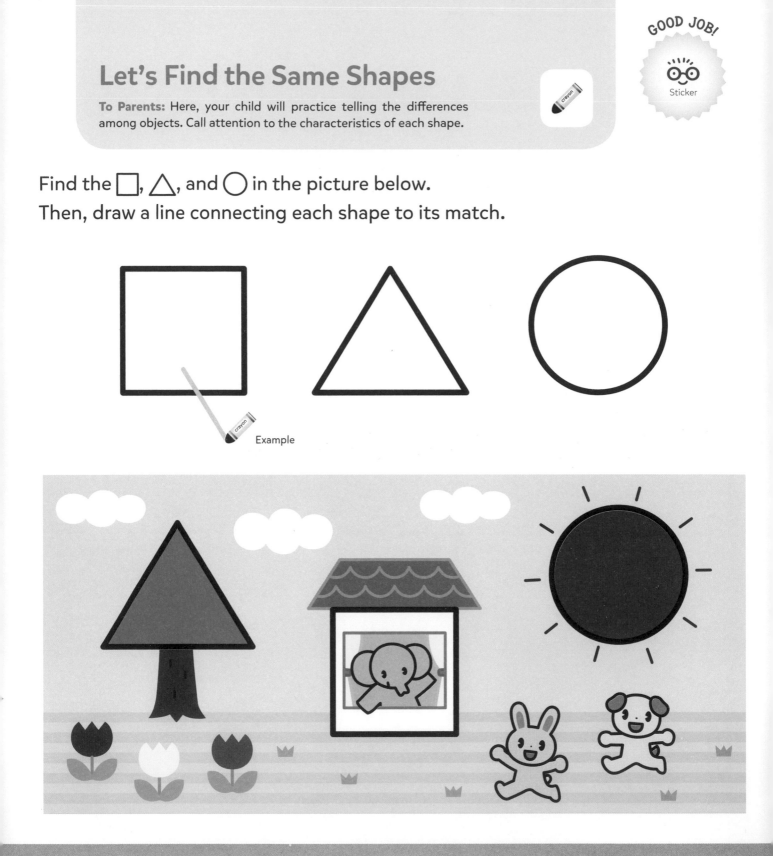

Example

Glue

Let's Match Parts to Wholes

To Parents: With this activity, your child will practice matching a part with its whole. Call attention to the different shapes and colors in each picture to help your child find similarities.

GOOD JOB!

Sticker

Look at the pictures in each ◯. Each contains a part of one of the pictures on the right. Draw a line to connect each part with its picture.

Example

Let's Find the Matching Hamsters

To Parents: This activity focuses on noting the differences among objects. If your child does not recognize the pairs right away, call attention to the different characteristics and colors of the hamsters.

GOOD JOB!

Sticker

Find the hamsters that are the same.

Draw a line to connect them.

Example

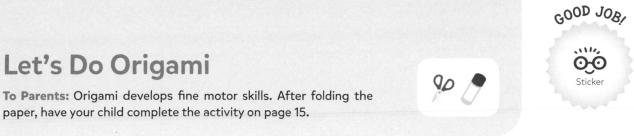

GOOD JOB!
Sticker

Let's Do Origami

To Parents: Origami develops fine motor skills. After folding the paper, have your child complete the activity on page 15.

Make the 2 fish and glue them to page 15.

• How to Fold •

Cut along the thick gray lines to make two squares.

Fold one of them in half.
(– – – – Line 1)

Fold

Fold both sides in.
(·–·–·– Line 2)

Fold

Fold

Flip the folded shape over.

Repeat for the other square.

Line2

Line1

Line2

Line1

Line2

Line1

Line2

Line1

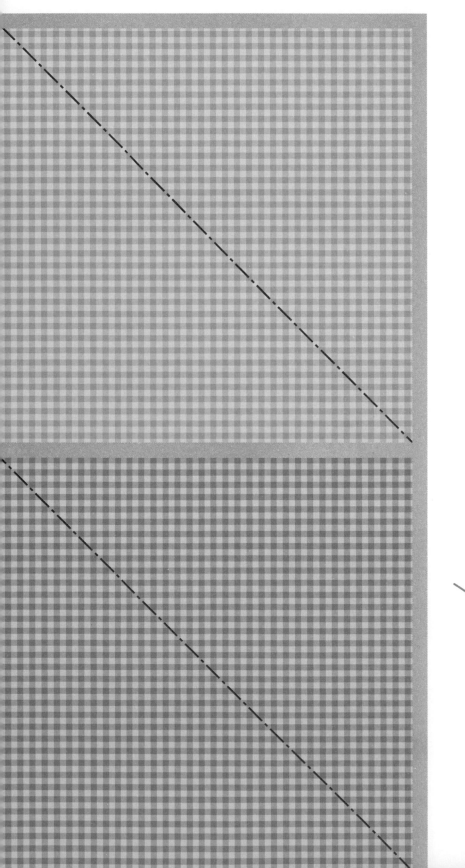

Glue each fish you made onto its matching shape on page 15.

Let's Glue the Fish in Place

To Parents: This activity exercises fine motor and decision-making skills. Call attention to the shapes of the two fish from page 13 to help your child glue each fish to its matching shape.

Glue the 2 fish you made from page 13 to the matching shapes.

Let's Find the Biggest Treats

To Parents: In this activity, your child will focus on the size differences among objects. Extend the activity by asking your child to find the smallest object in each group.

Color the ◯ under the biggest ice cream and under the biggest cupcake.

Let's Play a Jumping Game

To Parents: This jumping game exercises gross motor and decision-making skills. Read the instructions and praise your child upon completion of each task.

GOOD JOB!

Sticker

Cut out the strips. Then, choose a strip and do the activity on the strip.

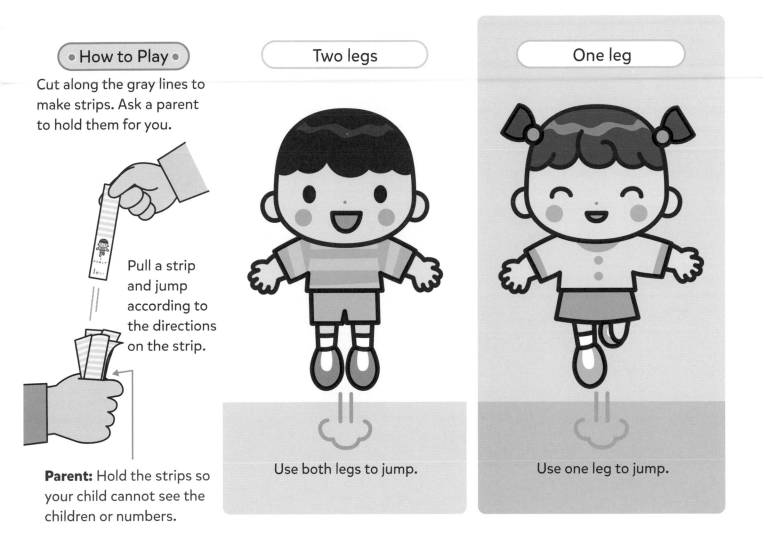

• **How to Play** •

Cut along the gray lines to make strips. Ask a parent to hold them for you.

Pull a strip and jump according to the directions on the strip.

Parent: Hold the strips so your child cannot see the children or numbers.

Two legs

Use both legs to jump.

One leg

Use one leg to jump.

Use both legs — 3 times

Use both legs — 2 times

Use both legs — 1 time

Use one leg — 3 times

Use one leg — 2 times

Use one leg — 1 time

Let's Trace the Lines

To Parents: Drawing curved lines helps build handwriting skills. After your child traces the lines, a snail and a cake appear. Ask your child what the images are.

GOOD JOB!

Sticker

Trace the ▪ ▪ ▪ from ➡ to ➡ to finish each picture. What did you draw?

Let's Find the End of the Maze

To Parents: Your child will practice using reasoning and problem-solving skills to complete this maze. Help him or her draw a path through the maze without hitting a dead end.

Help the puppy find its doghouse. Draw a line from ➡ to ➡.

Let's Find the End of the Maze

To Parents: To get through this maze, your child will use reasoning and problem-solving skills. Matching the stickers to the shadows lets children practice matching similar objects. And placing the stickers on the page develops fine motor skills.

Draw a line from ➡ to ➡.

Put the 2 stickers on the shadows that are the same shape.

Let's Use Insect Stickers

To Parents: This activity builds fine motor skills. Your child should feel free to put the stickers anywhere on the tree (the trunk, branches, or leaves).

Sticker

Put the insect stickers on the tree.

Example

Let's Make Shadow Puppets

To Parents: In this activity, your child will practice expressing mental pictures. Making shadow puppets also develops fine motor skills. Use the light from the sun or a flashlight to make shadow puppets.

GOOD JOB!
Sticker

Make shadow puppets with your hands.

Fox
Touch your thumb and two middle fingers together. Straighten your index and pinky fingers. Adjust your hand to make the best fox shadow you can.

Yelp yelp

Move your wrist to see what happens.
Make the sound a fox makes.

Bird
Put one thumb over the other. Extend your other fingers and keep them close together. Bend your fingers to imitate the flapping of a bird's wings.

Flap flap

Moving your fingers will make it look like a bird is flying.

Let's Find Hidden Objects

To Parents: Your child can exercise his or her observational skills by finding the objects hidden in the picture.

Examine the objects in the box. Find each object hidden in the picture below. Draw a line to connect each object in the box with its matching picture.

Example

Let's Find the Hidden Numbers

To Parents: In this activity, your child will use his or her observational skills to find hidden objects.

Find the numbers 1, 2, and 3 hidden in the picture.
Draw a ◯ around each number.

Let's Find the Differences

To Parents: Here, your child will practice carefully comparing pictures. If your child cannot find all of the differences, go over each feature together.

Find the 3 differences between the breakfast pictures.
Draw a ◯ around each difference in the breakfast on the bottom.

Let's Finish the Picture

To Parents: This activity builds spatial reasoning skills. Guide your child to pay attention not only to the content of the pictures, but also to the shapes of the puzzle pieces.

Look at the puzzle pieces. Where do they belong in the picture below?
Draw lines to show where the pieces belong.

Example

Let's Find Shapes and Colors

To Parents: In this activity, your child will practice recognizing different shapes and colors. When your child has finished coloring, ask what the object is.

Color **red** the shapes that contain a ■. Color **green** the shapes that contain a ●.
Color **brown** the shapes that contain a ▲. What picture do you see?

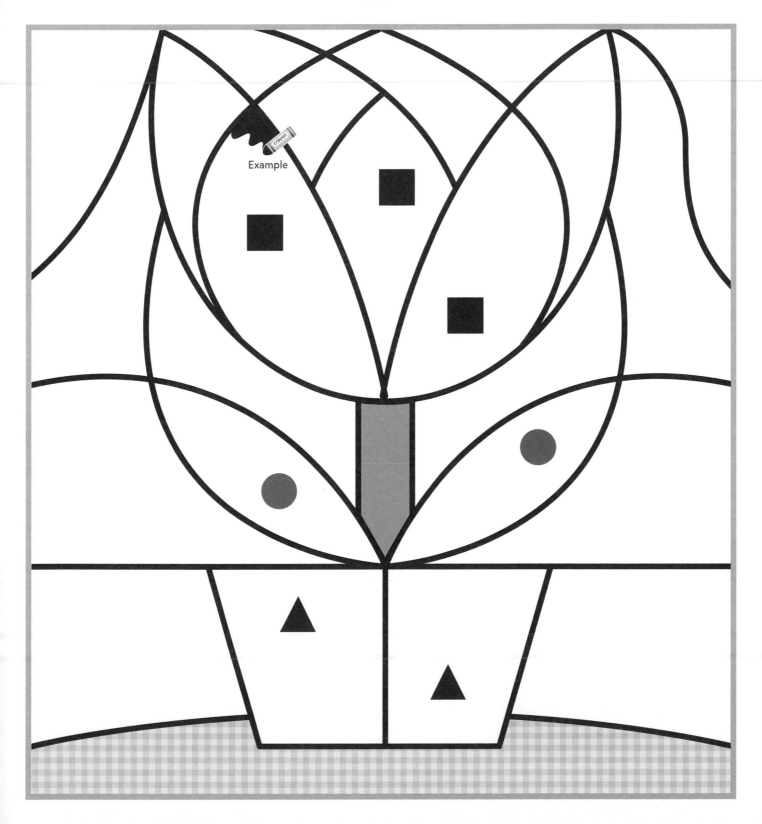

Let's Find the Matching Vehicle

To Parents: In this activity, your child will practice matching a shadow with its picture. Guide your child to look at the shapes in the shadow and compare them to the color pictures.

GOOD JOB!

Sticker

Which vehicle matches the shadow in the box? Draw a ◯ around it.

• Example •

Let's Remember the Picture

To Parents: This activity exercises memory. Once your child folds the paper, do not open it until he or she has circled an answer on the folded page.

First, cut along the gray line. Then, look at the picture and try to memorize it. After 10 seconds, fold up the page along the dotted line and answer the question.

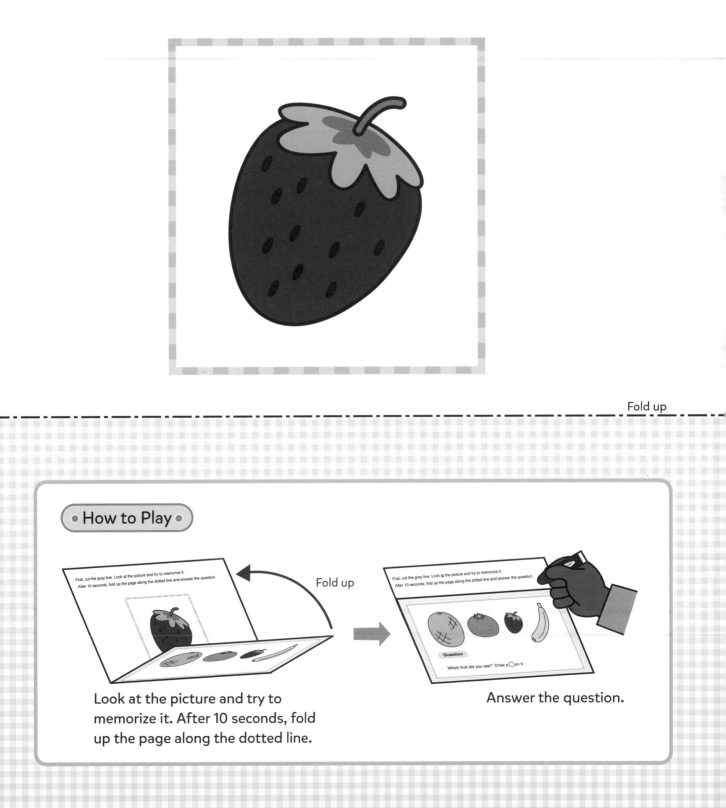

Fold up

• How to Play •

Fold up

Look at the picture and try to memorize it. After 10 seconds, fold up the page along the dotted line.

Answer the question.

Let's Play Airplane

To Parents: Here, your child will practice mimicking something. Have your child extend his or her arms out to the sides for better balance.

Pretend to be an airplane. Ask a parent to help you.

Airplane

Parents: Lie flat on your back with your legs bent, as shown in the picture. Your child should lie on top of your bent legs. Hold your child's hands firmly and move your legs left and right to mimic airplane movement.

Make airplane sounds.

Hold hands firmly.

Vroom vroom

Which fruit did you see? Draw a ◯ around it.

Question

Let's Give the Cow Its Spots

To Parents: Decorating an object with stickers builds fine motor skills and exercises creativity. Your child may put the stickers anywhere on the cow's body.

Sticker

Put the stickers on the cow's body to give it spots.

• Example •

Let's Find the End of the Maze

To Parents: This activity builds problem-solving skills and develops the skills needed for good handwriting. Remind your child to be careful when drawing a line through the narrow paths of the maze.

Draw a path through the maze from ➡ to ➡.

Let's Find the End of the Maze

To Parents: This activity builds problem-solving skills and develops the skills needed for good handwriting. Encourage your child to complete the maze without crossing any lines.

Draw a path through the maze from 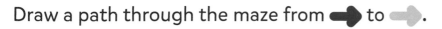 to .

Let's Color the Koala

To Parents: Here, your child will practice recognizing colors she or he might see in nature. Ask your child to choose what color to make the koala. Show pictures of a real koala if your child has never seen one before.

GOOD JOB!

Sticker

Color the koala.

Example

Let's Find Shapes and Colors

To Parents: This activity focuses on recognizing shapes and colors and noticing the differences among objects. Encourage your child to color inside the lines.

Let's color the balloons. Color **green** the balloon with a ◯. Color **red** the one with a ▢. Color **yellow** the one with a ♡. And color **blue** the one with a △.

Let's Match Parts to Wholes

To Parents: Here, your child will match parts with their wholes. Call attention to the details, such as the shape of the tail, to help your child find each match.

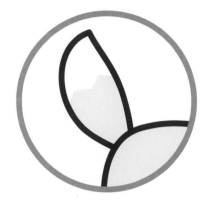

Each ◯ picture shows a different animal's tail.
Find the animal that matches each tail below. Draw a line to connect them.

Example

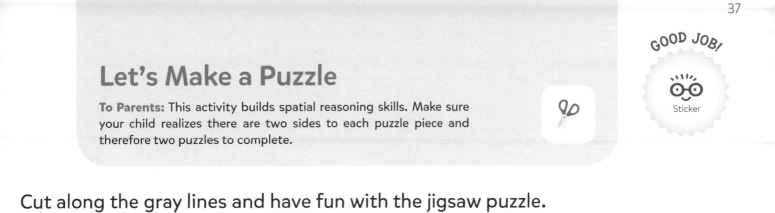

Let's Make a Puzzle

To Parents: This activity builds spatial reasoning skills. Make sure your child realizes there are two sides to each puzzle piece and therefore two puzzles to complete.

GOOD JOB!

Sticker

Cut along the gray lines and have fun with the jigsaw puzzle.

How to Play

Cut the paper into pieces, and shuffle the pieces. Then, put the picture together. You can make 2 different pictures.

Let's Find the Differences

To Parents: In this activity, your child will practice finding differences between two similar pictures. Ask your child to look carefully at each picture. Provide hints if needed.

GOOD JOB!

Sticker

Find the 3 differences between the top picture and the bottom picture.

Draw a ◯ around each difference in the picture on the bottom.

Let's Group the Objects

To Parents: This activity invites your child to categorize objects. After your child circles an object, ask for the reason behind the choice.

Find the object that does not belong in each group.

Draw a ◯ around it.

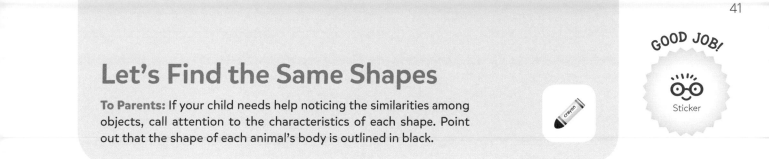

Let's Find the Same Shapes

To Parents: If your child needs help noticing the similarities among objects, call attention to the characteristics of each shape. Point out that the shape of each animal's body is outlined in black.

GOOD JOB!

Sticker

Look at the shape of each sea creature's body. Find the shapes on the right that match. Draw a line to connect each match.

Example

42

Let's Find the Longer Train

To Parents: This activity builds length-perception skills. Encourage your child to look at the entire length to determine which train is longer instead of counting train cars.

GOOD JOB!
Sticker

Look at each set of trains. Which train is longer in each set?
Color the ◯ next to the longer train.

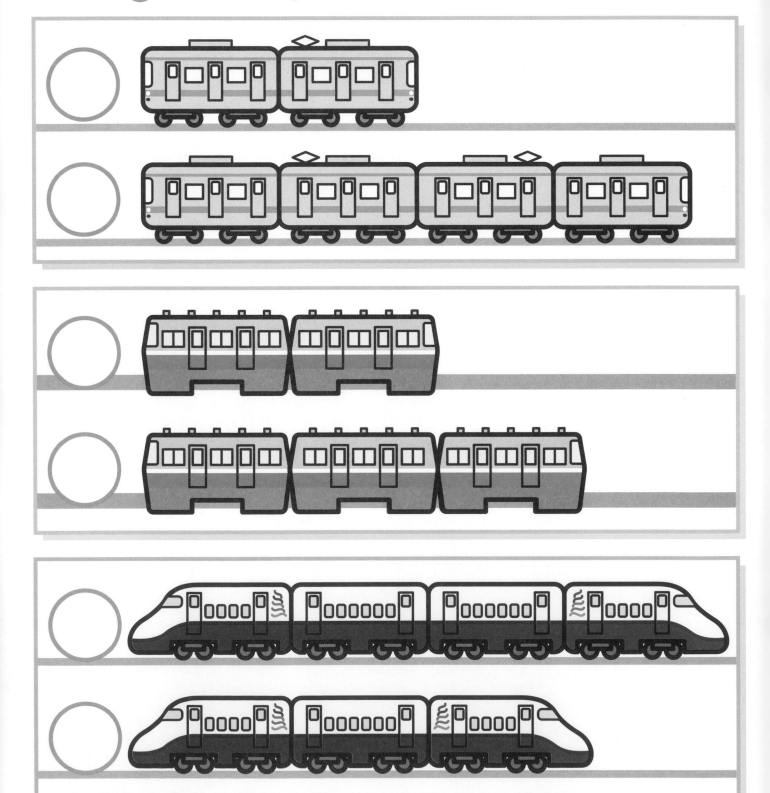

Let's Glue the Pajamas in Place

To Parents: With this activity, your child will practice manners, while building fine motor skills.

Cut out the pajamas along the gray lines. Glue them to the boy and girl.

Then say, "Good night."

Let's Find the End of the Maze

To Parents: Doing mazes helps build problem-solving skills and the skills needed for good handwriting.

crayon

Draw a line from  to ➡.

Glue

Glue

Let's Find the Hidden Letters

To Parents: In this activity, your child will sharpen his or her observational skills, while spotting hidden objects. The style of the letters might make them difficult to find. Encourage your child to carefully examine the picture, one area at a time.

Look at the picture below. Find the hidden letters A, B, C, and D.
Draw a line to connect each letter to its match.

Example

A   B   C   D

Let's Find the Matching Glasses

To Parents: This activity focuses on seeing the similarities and differences among objects. If your child is having a hard time finding the matches, call attention to the colors and shapes of the glasses.

Look at each pair of glasses and find its match.

Draw a line to connect the matching pairs of glasses.

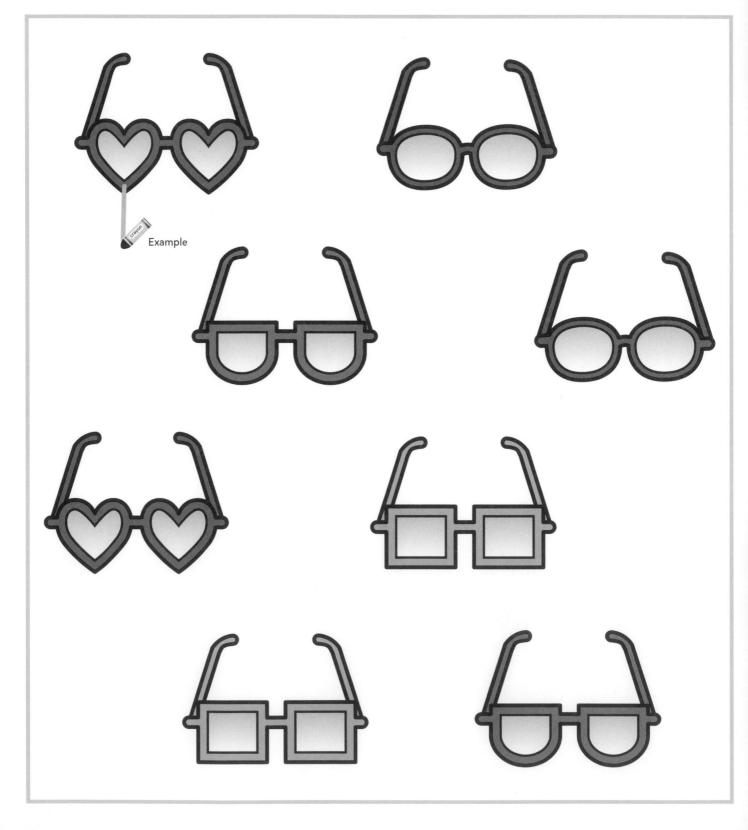

Example

Let's Match Parts to Wholes

To Parents: Here, your child will practice matching a part with its whole. Call attention to the details, such as shapes or colors, and help your child determine where each piece belongs.

Look at the pictures in each ◯. Each contains a part of one of the pictures on the right. Draw a line to connect each part with its picture.

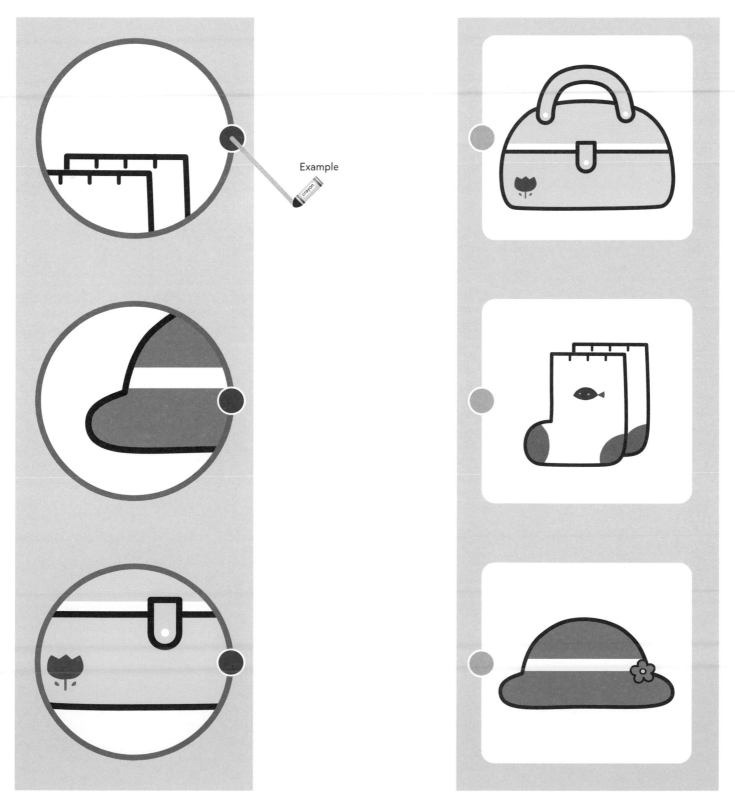

Example

GOOD JOB!

Sticker

48

Let's Draw a Picture

To Parents: Drawing pictures encourages creativity. Do not worry if your child's snowman does not match the example. Let your child draw freely.

Draw a snowman. Use the stickers to give your snowman a face and hands. Try using the bucket sticker for a hat.

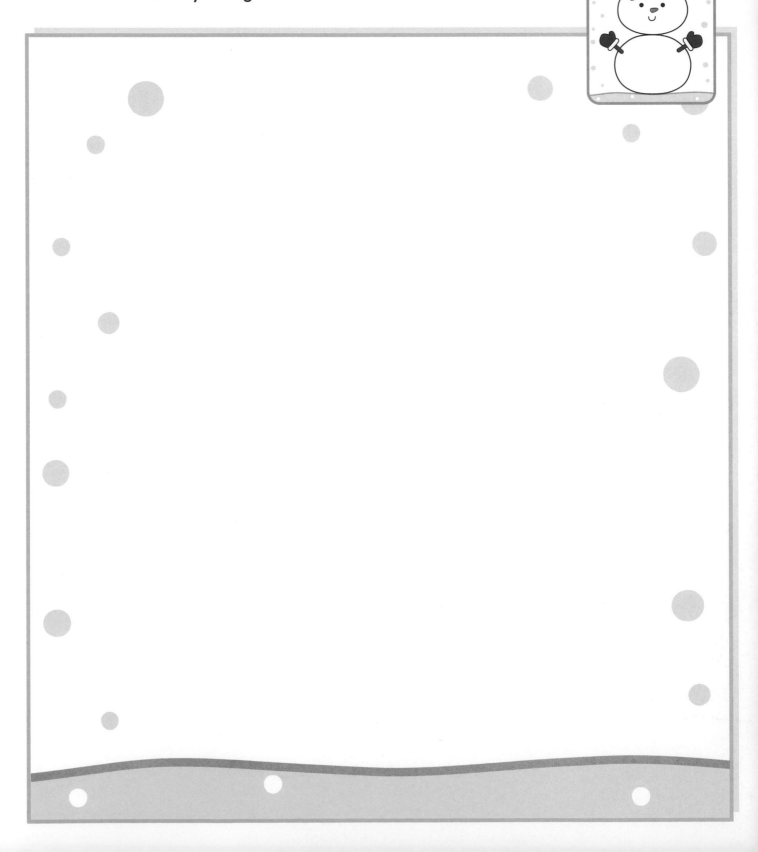

Let's Make Crafts

To Parents: Cutting and folding build fine motor skills. Ask your child what else she or he might like on the sandwich.

Let's make sandwiches.

• How to Make •

Cut along the gray lines to make food for the sandwiches.

Fold each square piece of paper in half to make a triangle.

★Read "How to Play" on page 50.

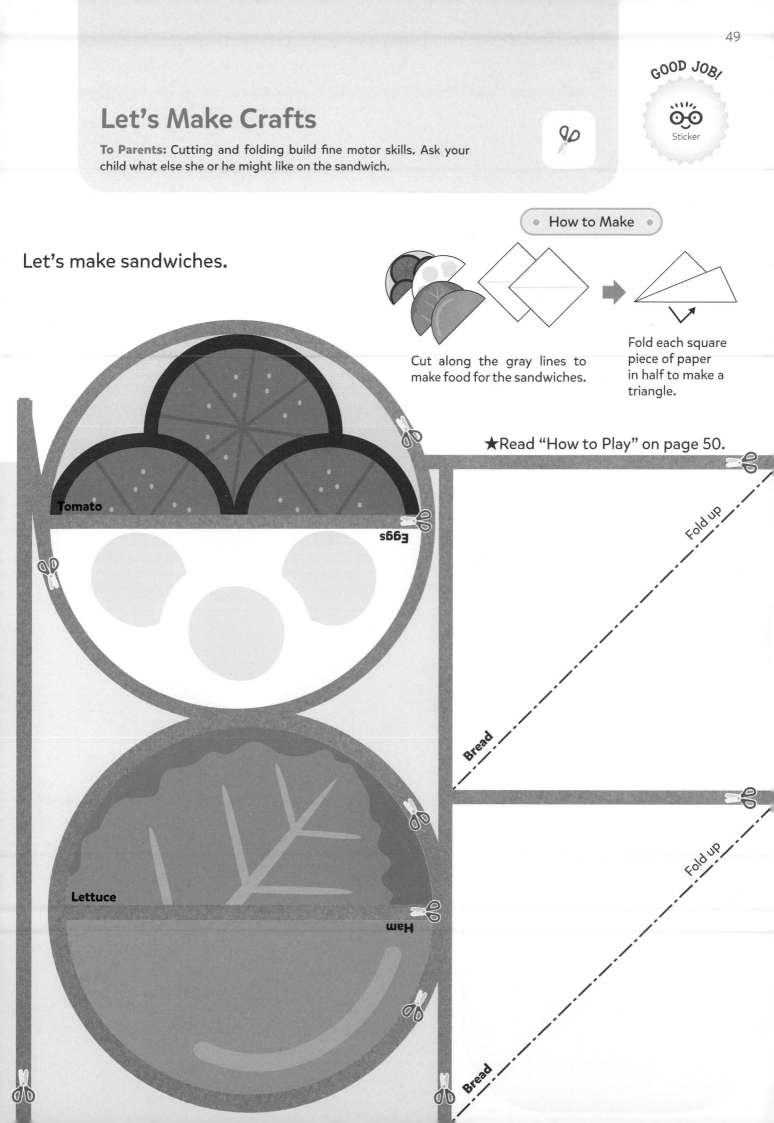

Tomato

Eggs

Lettuce

Ham

Bread

Fold up

Fold up

Bread

50

• How to Play •

Put any food you like in the bread to make a sandwich.

Pretend to eat what you just made.

Let's eat.

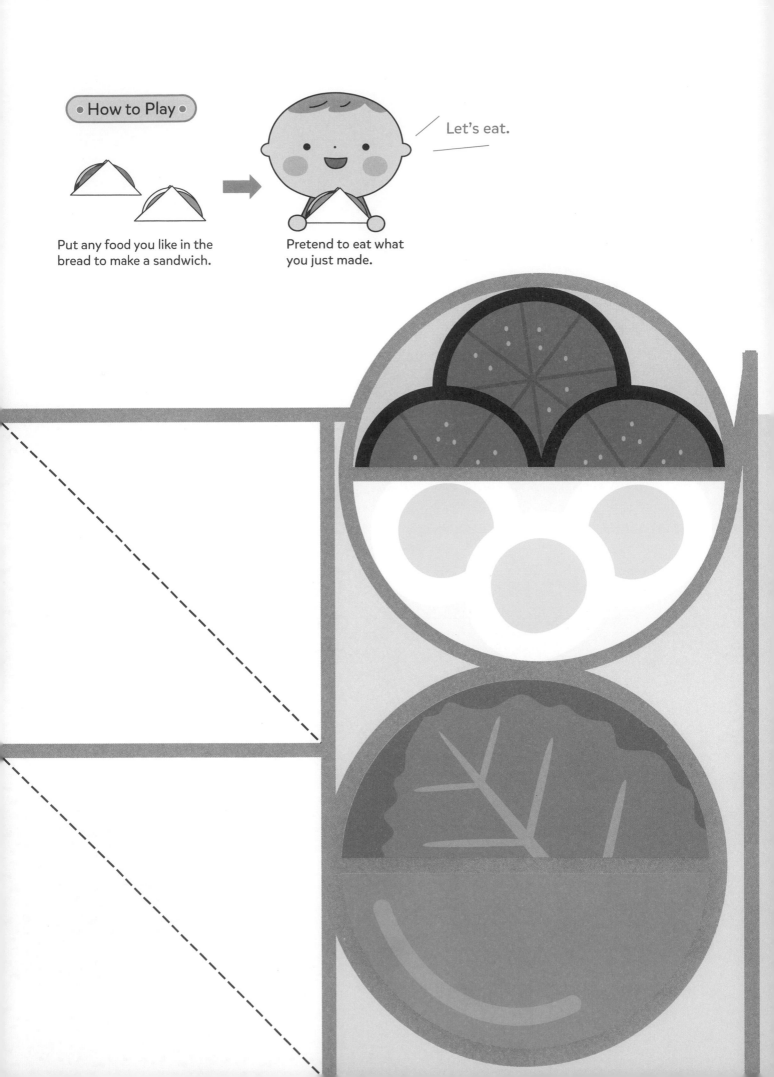

Let's Remember the Picture

To Parents: This activity exercises memory. Encourage your child to answer the question before looking at the basket of fruit again.

First, cut along the gray line. Look at the picture and try to memorize it. After 10 seconds, fold up the page along the dotted line and answer the question.

Fold up

Look at the picture and try to memorize it. After 10 seconds, fold up the page along the dotted line.

Answer the question.

Let's Play

To Parents: In this game, your child will practice expressing mental images. Once children understand how to play the game, let them come up with their own animals.

Imagine you are inside an egg. When the egg breaks apart, what will come out? Pretend to be that animal. Then, try again as another animal.

• How to Play •

Get a bath towel or blanket.

Cover your body with the blanket and pretend to be an egg that is hatching.

A penguin is born.

I'm a penguin.

A turtle is born.

I'm a turtle.

• Question •

Which fruit was in the basket? Draw a ◯ around the answer.

Let's Find the Hidden Animals

To Parents: This activity focuses on observational skills and locating hidden objects. Finding the hippopotamus and alligator might be difficult.

GOOD JOB!

Sticker

Animals are hiding in the jungle. Find the animals in the ◯ on the bottom. Then, draw a line to connect each match.

Example

Let's Find Matching Sweets

To Parents: This activity focuses on distinguishing characteristics. The changes in the size and positioning of the sweets can make this activity difficult. Give hints if your child needs them.

GOOD JOB!
Sticker

There are sweets hidden around the castle.
Find each sweet and draw a line to its match on the bottom.

Example

Let's Group the Objects

To Parents: This activity helps your child better understand the world. Guide your child to determine which store sells the items in the cutouts. By cutting and pasting, your child is also practicing fine motor skills.

Cut along the gray lines. Find the store that sells each group of items. Glue the items to the matching store.

Let's Color the Vehicles

To Parents: Guide your child to color the fire engine red, but to color the other vehicles any color. In this activity, your child will demonstrate an understanding of the differences among colors.

crayon

Color all the vehicles.

Example

Glue   Glue   Glue   Glue

Let's Remember the Picture

To Parents: This game exercises memory. Encourage your child to answer the question before unfolding the paper.

First, cut along the gray line. Look at the picture and try to remember it. After 10 seconds, fold up the page along the dotted line and answer the question.

Fold up

• How to Play •

Fold up

Look at the picture and try to remember it. After 10 seconds, fold up the page along the dotted line.

Answer the question.

Let's Draw Tulips

To Parents: Show your child pictures of tulips. In this activity, your child will choose how to draw a specific object. This exercise encourages creativity.

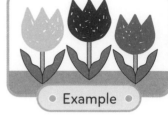

Draw tulips on each of the stems.

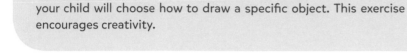
Example

Which animals were not in the picture? Draw a ◯ around the answers.

Question

* The answers are two different kinds of animals.

Let's Draw Matching Pictures

To Parents: This activity encourages attention to detail and builds handwriting skills. After finishing the activity, ask your child to compare the drawing to the example to check for accuracy.

Draw lines from ● to ● to make a picture that matches each example.

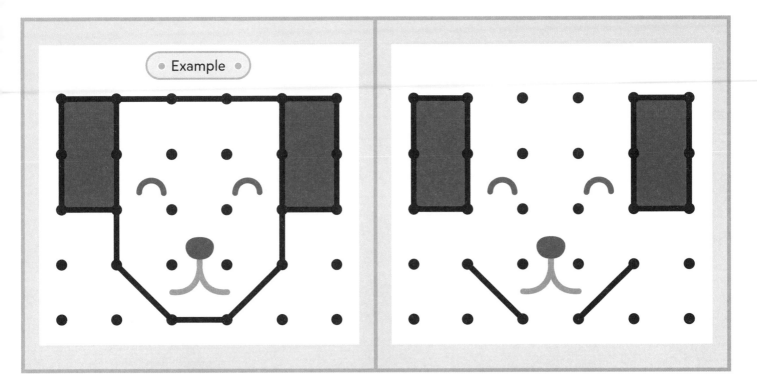

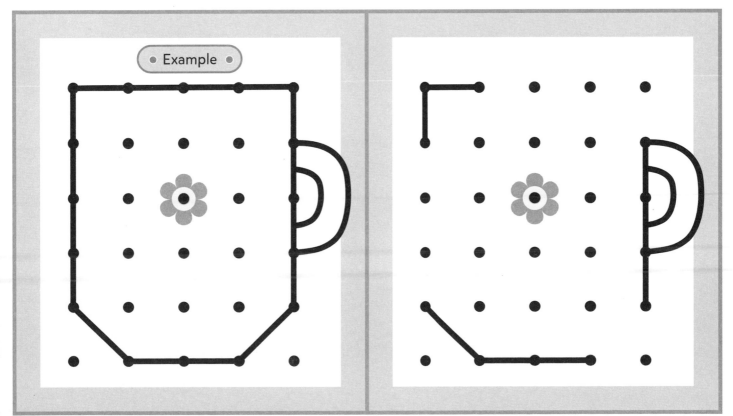

Let's Learn Life Cycles

To Parents: This activity helps your child better understand the world. Explain that some living things change when they grow into adults. Ask your child to name each living thing.

GOOD JOB!
Sticker

Look at each living thing on the left. Match each one with what it grows into on the right. Draw a line to connect each match.

Example

Let's Find the Matching Outfit

To Parents: Here, your child will practice finding the differences between two pictures. The two girls look similar, so make sure your child pays attention to the details.

Which girl is wearing the same clothes as in the 〇 ?
Fill in the 〇 below the girl.

Let's Color the Picture

To Parents: Have your child make a small mark on each area that has a heart before coloring it in fully. In this activity, your child will practice finding the differences among objects.

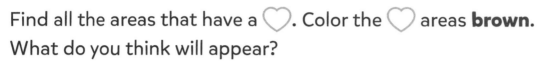

Find all the areas that have a ♡. Color the ♡ areas **brown**.
What do you think will appear?

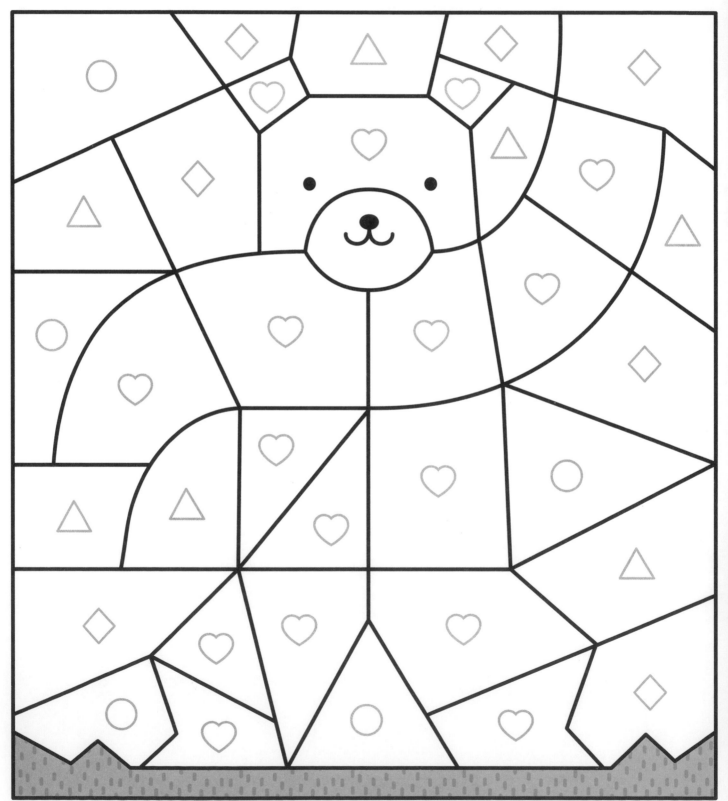

Answers for pages 1 to 38

To Parents: These images show the answers for pages 1 to 38. Use them to check the answers with your child.

p. 1

*The answer above is just an example. As long as the cakes are placed inside the box, they could be in any order.

p. 3

p. 4

p. 6

p. 7

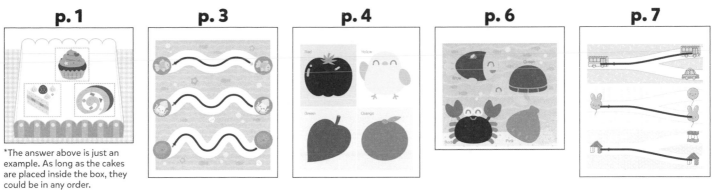

p. 8

p. 10

p. 11

p. 12

p. 15

p. 16

p. 18

p. 19

p. 20

p. 23

p. 24

p. 25

p. 26

p. 27

Tulip

p. 28

p. 29, 30

p. 32

p. 33

p. 35

p. 36

*There are no answers for pages 2, 5, 9, 13–14, 17, 21, 22, 31, 34, 37, and 38.

Answers for pages 39 to 62

To Parents: These images show the answers for pages 39 to 62. Use them to check the answers with your child.

p. 39

p. 40

p. 41

p. 42
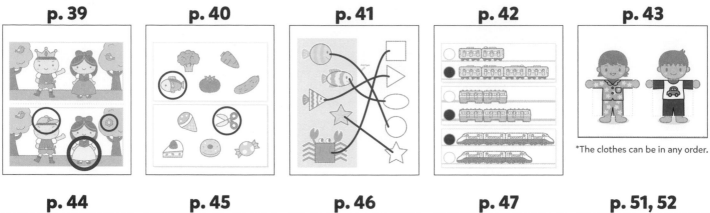

p. 43

*The clothes can be in any order.

p. 44
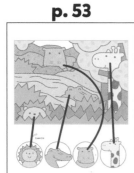

p. 45

p. 46
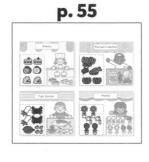

p. 47

p. 51, 52
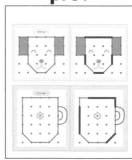

p. 53

p. 54

p. 55

p. 57, 58
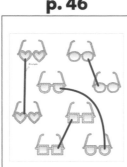
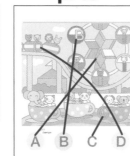

p. 59

p. 60

p. 61

p. 62

Bear

*There are no answers for pages 48, 49–50, 52, 56, and 58.

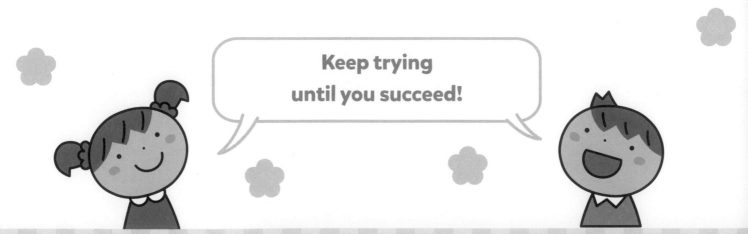

Keep trying until you succeed!

WIPE-CLEAN
Game Board
You can draw and erase, again and again.

To Parents: Drawing encourages creativity. Have your child use water-based markers on the wipe-clean side of the board. When your child is finished drawing, erase the board with a damp cloth.

Draw a picture of someone you like.

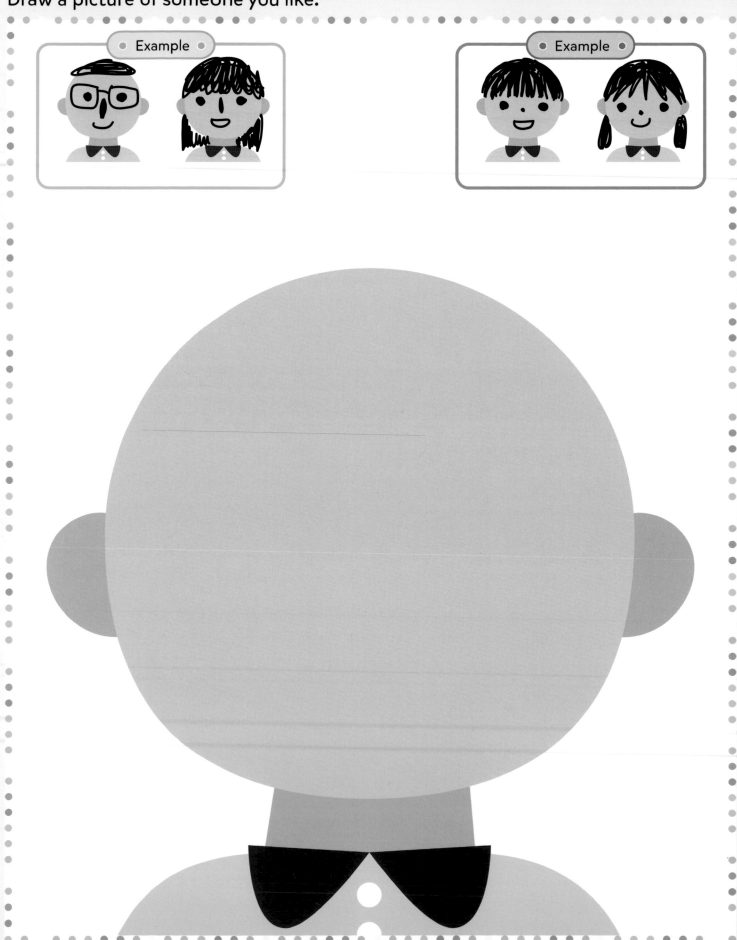

Example

Example

Let's Jump!

To Parents: In this activity, your child will build gross motor skills and practice comparing distances.

How far can you jump?

To Parents: Before your child jumps, mark where he or she is standing. Then, measure at least two jumps. Ask, "Which jump was the longest?"

Put your feet together, count "One, two, three!" and jump forward.

One, two, three!

As you jump, bring your hands forward to help you jump farther.

How high can you jump?

To Parents: When your child jumps to reach your hand, keep raising your hand higher as an added challenge.

Ask a parent to hold out his or her hand. Jump up to touch it.

One, two, three!

Bend your knees before you jump. It will help you jump higher.